Great Chalfield Manor

WILTSHIRE

A souvenir guide

![National Trust] **National Trust**

LIVING AT GREAT CHALFIELD

by Robert Floyd

The manor, its active parish church, garden, houses, woods and farmland, which form the small estate of Great Chalfield, are gems in a rare and peaceful setting. The manor is both a beloved family home to our three sons and our dogs, and a focus for a rural community. Recreation is central in this beautiful place – a joy to some 20,000 visitors each year, including walkers, plant hunters and monthly meetings of the Quiet Garden.

Over the last twenty years, my wife Patsy and our gardener Neil have replanted and brought borders to life, in keeping with Alfred Parsons's garden designs for my grandfather. Now there are colour and interest in spring, summer and autumn, as well as in the changing light of winter.

Our public footpath network is much improved by diversions in 1992, with three new footbridges across the Chalfield brook thanks to the West Wilts Ramblers. Walks to The Courts at Holt offer delightful glimpses of woodland both old and new and of the wildlife celebrated in Andrew Taylor's 1999 stained-glass window for the church. My heart leaps at the brilliant blue dash of kingfishers along the Saxon mill leat, which feeds the Upper and Lower Moats. Running water has always been central to the spirit of Great Chalfield.

Each generation subtly changes the emphasis. For our part, we have a regime of opening windows in summer so that the whole house is warm, and the days of walls running with condensation are now very rare. Warm chimneys attract jackdaws, and once a barn owl in the Hall. I envied his elegant swallow dive through the window bars into the orchard.

We hope you will return again and again at different seasons to share the enjoyment of our home, which was judged by *Country Life* magazine to be among the six finest manor houses in England.

Top One of the many streams that flow through the garden

Above The family's riding boots on the stairs

Left The Great Hall

Opposite The Summer Border is planted with irises and hardy geraniums

GREAT CHALFIELD MANOR

THE MATCHLESS MANOR HOUSE

Great Chalfield is still an isolated hamlet set in rich farming country. You approach from the north along a quiet country lane, and your first view of the house is perfect: a careful composition of gables and Gothic windows, nestling next to the little parish church, and all reflected in the remains of the old moat.

Above This ornate oriel window marks the Solar, used by Tropnell and honoured guests

Below J.C. Buckler's watercolour of the north front and the church in 1823

The North Front

The entrance front has changed little since it was built in 1467–80 by Thomas Tropnell as a triumphant statement in stone of his rise to local eminence after a lifetime of hard work. The house is laid out symmetrically with deceptive simplicity. The high-roofed Great Hall in the centre is flanked to left and right by wings set at right angles that contain the main living rooms. The most important chambers are on the first floor, indicated by the grand bay windows. To the right is the long kitchen range, which ends with the 14th-century gatehouse.

Great Chalfield was built at a time of turmoil, and the entrance courtyard would originally have been less open, defended by a moat and a high outer wall with semicircular bastions, of which only the lower courses survive.

Below The Entrance Porch

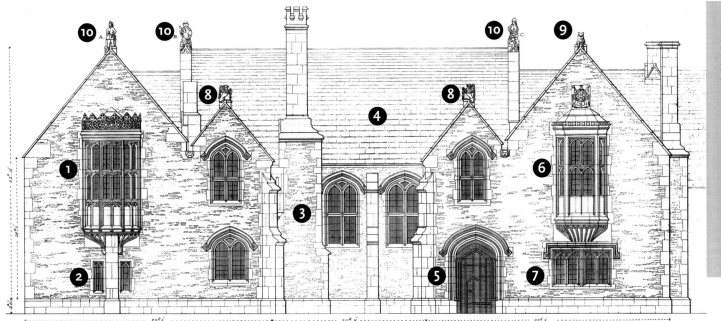

The Entrance Porch

A broad Gothic archway welcomes visitors into the porch with its fine vaulted ceiling, which matches those in the bays at the upper (east) end of the Great Hall. Amazingly, the original oak door has survived centuries of strife. To 'bar the door' completely, you slide a timber let into the wall from one side to the other. If you want to let just one person in at a time, you open only the low inner 'wicket' door.

On the corbel (bracket) to the right of the door, an angel holds up the Tropnell coat of arms. A spyhole (or squint) provides a view from the Dining Room into the Porch.

Messages in stone

The façade is composed in an architectural 'language' that the medieval visitor would have readily understood.

1 **Best bay window**
Solar/Great Chamber used by Tropnell and honoured guests

2 **Small windows**
Protect valuables in Groined Room

3 **Great Hall chimneystack**
Symbolises warmth

4 **Great Hall**
Grandest room has highest roof

5 **Porch**
Wide archway welcomes visitors

6 **Second-best bay window**
Principal family apartment with family coat of arms above window

7 **Best ground-floor windows**
Parlour

8 **Griffin holding Tropnell arms**

9 **Lion** (from Percy arms)

10 **Knight in armour**

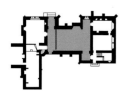

TOUR OF THE HOUSE

Great Chalfield may look little changed from Tudor times. In fact, its present appearance owes much to sympathetic restoration in the early 20th century by Sir Harold Brakspear for Robert Fuller, who furnished it with period furniture, Flemish tapestries and fine eastern rugs. Like nearby Westwood Manor (also National Trust), it is an important example of the Edwardian taste for the ancient English manor house.

THE GREAT HALL

This was the largest room in a medieval house and its social and emotional heart. The great fireplace is still in regular use and draws well. But this Great Hall also looks forward in its arrangement and proportions. It is not open to the rafters, like a traditional hall, but has a ceiling. The 'high' (family) end is indicated, not by a dais, but by matching bays with vaulted ceilings decorated with the Tropnell arms.

In 1838 the Great Hall was divided in two by a mezzanine floor, but this was removed by Brakspear in 1905–12.

Below The Great Hall today

Screens passage

You enter in the traditional fashion at the 'low' (servants') end through a screens passage. However, the present screen is an Edwardian replacement, based on T.L. Walker's careful 1836 drawings of the original, which was removed in the mid-19th century to make way for a staircase. The minstrels' gallery and doorway above are Edwardian additions.

Ceiling

The ceiling is the original, but in medieval times it would have been richly painted and gilded (traces of red ochre pigment survive). During the 1838 alterations it also lost the wooden bosses and plaster ribs that had subdivided it. 130 years later, one of these plaster fragments was retrieved from the crypt of the Bishop's Palace at Wells (now on show in the dole cupboard). It bears Tropnell's double yoke badge, which is also painted on the ceiling, together with his motto in Old French, *Le jong tyra belement* ('The yoke draws well').

Floor

Major Fuller replaced the original flagstones with a sprung oak dance floor. Stone benches, which ran along the walls as in a cathedral chapterhouse, were removed after 1823 (a slot for the bench ends can still be seen to the left of the fireplace).

Furniture

The oak pieces were collected by the Fullers as appropriate furnishings for their ancient home and to create a comfortable sitting room. The small north Italian **writing-desk** is decorated with a painting of St Elizabeth bidding farewell to the Virgin Mary. The companion cedar **wedding chest** has an engraved outline of bride and groom on the front.

Tapestries

The 17th-century Antwerp tapestries depicting the Acts of the Apostles were designed by Abraham van Diepenbeck. They still bear the mark of Philip Wauters, a tapestry merchant through whose hands they passed. Major Fuller bought them in 1944 to decorate this room, with the encouragement of the National Trust's Historic Buildings Secretary, James Lees-Milne. New oak shutters made from estate timber reduce the amount of sunlight falling on the tapestries.

An ass of a bishop

In the wall above the minstrels' gallery a **stone face** laughs at two more masks at the opposite end of the Great Hall: a **bishop with a mitre** and a **king with asses' ears** (his crown has disappeared). Tropnell seems to be having a joke at the expense of Robert Wayville, Bishop of Salisbury, and his mistress, Constance Fitzwaryn. She was the widow of Sir Harry Percy, whose descendants Tropnell had ejected from Great Chalfield. The masks may also recall the words of the 12th-century scholar John of Salisbury: 'Rex illiteratus asinus coronatus' ('One might as well crown an ass as have an illiterate king').

Opposite The Great Hall in 1823; watercolour by J.C. Buckler (detail)

THE DINING ROOM

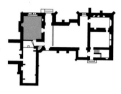

You would expect to find the servants' quarters here, but the medieval custom of eating communally in the Great Hall was dying out by Tropnell's time. He preferred to eat in private with his family in this room, which was his Parlour.

Right The Dining Room

Below The inlaid oak panelling in the Dining Room was put up about 1560

Ceiling and panelling

The plaster ceiling and oak panelling were added around 1560 by John Eyre, who had married Tropnell's great-granddaughter Ann in 1550. Their initials appear on the ceiling ribs and in the overmantel.

In the process of modernising the room, the Eyres covered up two of its most interesting medieval features – the mural and the squint, which offered Tropnell an advance sight of visitors arriving in the Porch.

Stone stairs lead up to an equally important room.

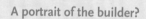

A portrait of the builder?

The late medieval wall-painting is hard to explain. It depicts a well-fed man seated in front of a red and white background which may be a ceremonial canopy. He is wearing a beaver hat and a coat trimmed with ermine, and carries a money bag. Is this prosperous gentleman Thomas Tropnell? It is quite possible, but at present unprovable. If it is, then this is the earliest known portrait of a commoner MP.

THE NORTH BEDROOM

This seems to have been the principal family room, balancing the Solar on the east side of the Great Hall. Its importance is indicated by the oriel window on the north side. In the traditional medieval fashion, the room is open to the rafters, which are mostly original.

Stained glass
In the upper left-hand light of the bay window are two birds holding a pious text: 'Love God, drede shame, desire worship and kepe thy name.' This is the only medieval glass to have survived the damage caused by the Parliamentary garrison during the Civil War.

Furnishings
The elaborately carved tester *bed* and other pieces are late 17th-century or later. The *curtains* were remade in 1973, retaining the Edwardian panels.

Below The North Bedroom

THE CLOSET

Adjoining the North Bedroom and immediately above the Entrance Porch is a little room which has probably always served as a dressing room. The little spiral staircase gave access to the roof of the Great Hall, and a matching stair descends to the closet in the Solar wing.

Bath
The Edwardian bath was introduced by the Fullers, but to conceal this modern intrusion, they panelled it in linenfold oak and gave it a wooden lid. When the Queen Mother visited in 1959, she noticed the bath. Unbeknown to her host, house guests had thrown all their clothes into it when getting ready for her arrival – much to her amusement, when all was revealed.

THE GROINED ROOM

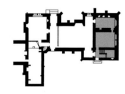

This room takes its name from the form of its vaulting, in which the various elements meet at a sharp edge, with no linking ribs. Tropnell would have used the room to store valuables such as silver, spices or legal documents. Hence, the small windows on the north side. (The large east window is an Edwardian addition.)

This part of the house was completely demolished in 1838, apart from the north wall. Brakspear carefully reconstructed it, using the original keystones (which he found discarded in the garden) to establish the form of the vaulting as recorded by T.L. Walker in 1836. Some of Brakspear's drawings for the house are displayed here.

Furniture

The fine early 16th-century French **cupboard** was bought by Robert Fuller in 1912 from J.S. Gardner of Maidenhead, who also supplied electric light fittings and lamps for the house.

The **moth collection** was largely made at Great Chalfield in the 1950s.

Below Views of the Solar

Return to the Great Hall, cross to the south-east bay and climb the Edwardian stairs to the Solar.

THE SOLAR

This was Tropnell's Solar or Great Chamber, where he would have entertained important guests. It is now used as a drawing room.

Brakspear rebuilt the room carefully following Walker's measured drawings, which record that the purlins and cross-braces had had decorative mouldings and so were meant to be seen. The most important surviving original feature is the very grand *bay window* in the north wall with its delicate fan vaulting. From here Tropnell could look out over the front courtyard and the church, to which he added the pretty little spire and belfry.

The *fireplace* was probably added in the 16th century by the Eyre family. Because it was not original, Walker dismissed it as 'a singular design of meretricious taste'. Brakspear had to reconstruct it from fragments unearthed in the farmer's rockery. The trumpeters' *banners* which bear Major Fuller's coat of arms were used when he was High Sheriff of Wiltshire in 1926.

Furniture
To the right of the fireplace, the oak *cupboard* with late 15th-century Gothic decorative doors and linenfold panels at the sides is the best piece of English furniture in the house. The walnut *piano* was a wedding present to Mabel Chappell from her family's firm, the music publisher Chappell & Co., on her marriage to Robert Fuller in 1911.

Textiles
The late 16th-century *tapestry* depicting *Hector bidding farewell to Andromache* (from Homer's Iliad) was made in Enghien in Belgium. It bears the mark of the van der Cammen family and was given with other tapestries for display at Great Chalfield by the Fullers' only child, Mary.

Top The border of the late 16th-century Flemish tapestry in the Solar
Right From the bay window you get a good view of the belfry and spire that Thomas Tropnell added to the church

Alfred Parsons (1847–1920) is best known as a landscape painter, who specialised in romantic watercolours of Cotswold gardens, but he also designed the gardens themselves, in a mellow Arts and Crafts manner.

Right One of the topiary yew 'houses' with the summer-house beyond

Opposite Parson's design of c.1907 for the paved walk and lavender borders

THE GARDEN

The garden was created at the same time as the restoration of the manor house and now provides the perfect complement to it — tranquil and lovingly tended. It lies mostly to the south and east of the house, sloping down to the stream which forms its southern boundary.

ALFRED PARSONS AT GREAT CHALFIELD

Tropnell's garden had long since disappeared by 1907, when Fuller commissioned the firm of Parsons, Partridge & Tudway to landscape the orchard, moat and stewponds around the house. Alfred Parsons supplied designs, for which he was paid in three instalments of 50 guineas.

Parsons lowered the forecourt by 18 inches and gravelled it to create a more imposing first view of the house and reduce damp from the moat. He paved the courtyard to the south of the house with a formal scheme of island beds. Parsons retained the late medieval feature of a large lawn or 'pleasaunce', which served as tennis courts surrounded by deep flower borders. New dry-stone walls replaced sloping banks to create terraces linked by flagstone paths. Vertical accents were provided by the now-substantial topiary yew 'houses' and a two-storey stone summer-house built by Brakspear beneath a now 100-year-old cedar, which closed the vista along the Top Terrace. The boundary walls were set under broad roll-top coping modelled on the traditional Cotswold form found in the churchyard. Walls near the house are flat-topped for sitting out. Parson's initial scheme was more elaborate, but Fuller reined him in, partly to keep costs down.

On Parsons's proposal for the circular pool between the yew houses, Fuller commented: 'The Italian design for this is very nice but I rather wanted to stick to purely British as far as possible.'

Planting began in 1910 (the budget was £100). Parsons incorporated the existing walnuts and medlars and added his favourite black mulberry, which now has to be supported on crutches. In keeping with his Arts and Crafts philosophy, he proposed mainly traditional native flowers, planted formally near the house, informally on the lower terraces. Parsons's rose garden and kitchen garden were grassed over in the 1960s to save money, but otherwise the planting is maintained in the Parsons spirit by Patsy Floyd and her team to a very high standard.

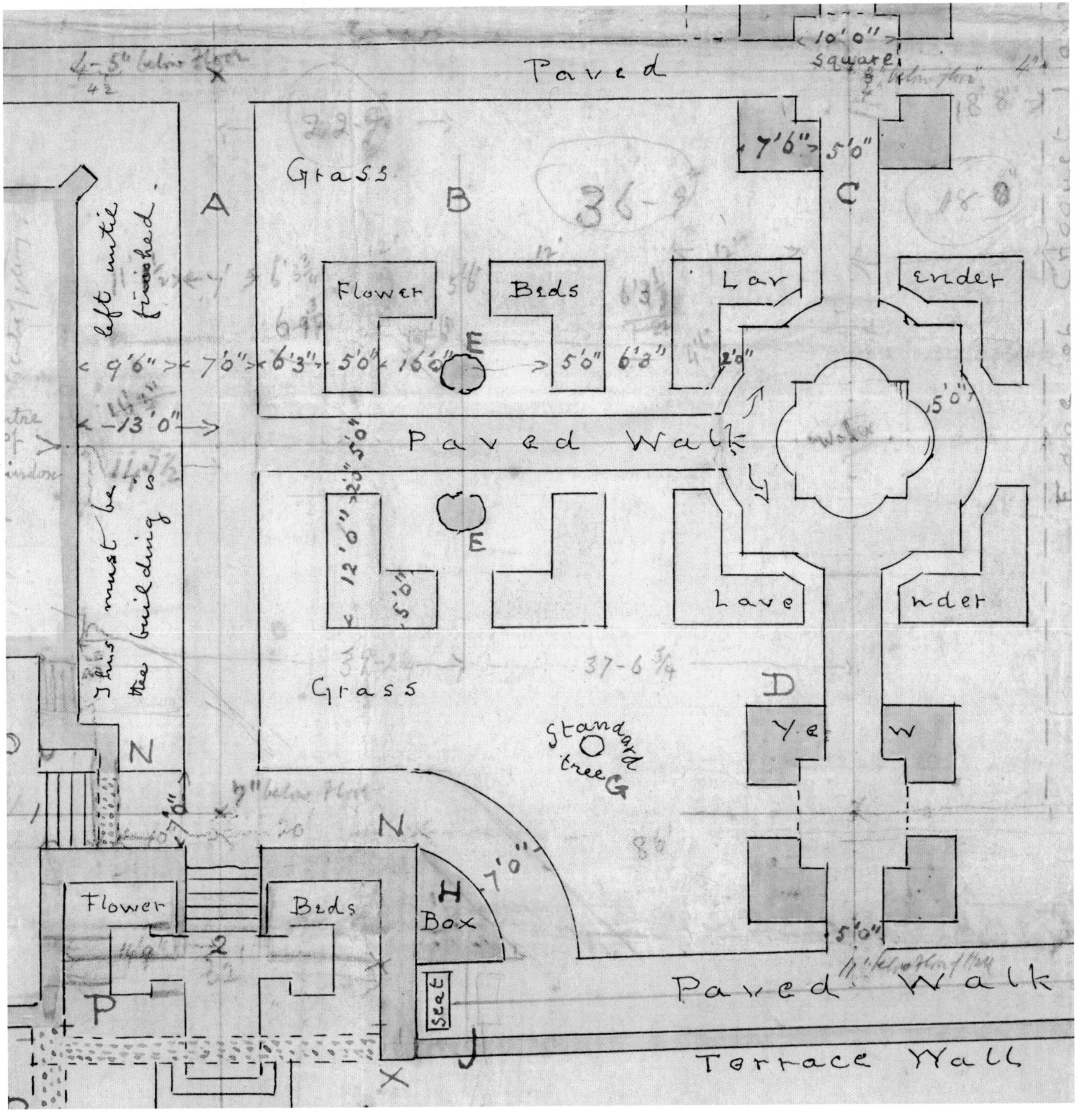

Paved

10'0" square

4-5" below floor
42

Grass

7'6" 5'0"

A   B   C

left until finished.

Flower   Beds   Lar   ender

9'6" 7'0" 6'3" 5'0" 16'0"   E   5'0" 6'3"   4' 2'0"   5'0"

13'0"

grass must be 14'3" to the building

Paved Walk   water

12'0" 20' 5'0"

5'0"   E

Lave   nder

Grass   37-6 3/4   D

standard
tree
G   Ye   w

N

7'0"   6" below floor
10

N

Flower   Beds   H
                       Box

7'0"
seat

P

Paved   Walk   5'0"

J

X

Terrace Wall

Old roses are, as one would expect, a feature of Great Chalfield. 'Bennett's Seedling' and the climber 'Madame Caroline Testout' are mixed with hybrid musk and modern shrub varieties to extend the flowering season. They fill the air with delicious scents. The delicate pink 'old blush China' grows on Mary Gibbons's 1832 grave in the churchyard.

Above Climbing roses on the half-timbered south-west wing

Opposite The garden slopes down from the house to the lower 'moat'

TOUR OF THE GARDEN

THE PAVED COURT

This courtyard with its central well was originally enclosed by a range of buildings on the south side, which were demolished before 1794. (Only the foundations survive as low garden walls.) The half-timbered wing was rebuilt by Fuller in 1910, incorporating one old window. The four beds are filled with the pink-flowered polyantha rose 'Nathalie Nypels'. *Campanula pyramidalis* and wild strawberries have self-seeded between the flagstones.

THE CHURCH BORDER

Aconites are followed by the blues of Ceanothus, Caryopteris and Delphinium with yellow Thalictrum – all at their best in June. Lupins, *Crambe cordifolia* and *Nepeta × faassenii* lead into Salvias interspersed with annuals such as Nicandra (the 'shoo fly' plant).

ALL SAINTS CHURCH

The church was built in the 14th century within the walls of the pre-Tropnell house and has always been closely linked to it. Around 1480 Tropnell added the *chapel* on the south side, with its fine stone screen (decorated with coats of arms celebrating Tropnell marriages) and murals depicting the martyrdom of St Catherine of Alexandria. He also built the picturesque *spire* and *bellcote*, and the *porch*. John Hall of Bradford-on-Avon gave the attractive three-decker *pulpit* in 1670. In 1775 Robert Neale added the *vestry*, and in 1912 the Fullers restored the whole building. The *organ case* was painted in 1914 by a Miss Maurice, who copied the saints from the 15th-century rood screen at Ranworth in Norfolk.

The vibrant *stained-glass window* in the Tropnell chapel illustrates the Parable of the Sower and includes wild flowers to be seen in the garden and surrounding farmland. It was designed in 1999 by the Wiltshire artist Andrew Taylor in memory of the Fullers' only child Mary and her husbands, John Boyle, who died in action near Anzio in 1944, and Charles Floyd, who founded the Wiltshire Wildlife Trust.

THE LAWN BORDER

Spring tulips flourish here in front of philadelphus and *Staphylea colchica*. The long, deep border is at its best in summer, when Italian white sunflowers, geraniums, artemisia and cosmos are a particular feature.

THE TOP TERRACE

The free-draining soil here favours osteospermums, rock roses and verbascums.

THE ASTER BORDER

Below the Top Terrace lies the Aster Border, where you can enjoy numerous cultivars of *Aster ericoides*. Maidenhair spleenwort ferns and ivy-leaved toadflax have established themselves in crevices in the dry-stone walls.

THE ORCHARD

In spring this is a mass of wild flowers, old varieties of narcissi and 'Queen of Night' tulips. They are followed in early summer by roses scrambling through the branches of the old apple trees. Parsons painted attractive watercolours of ancient apple trees blossoming above a froth of Queen Anne's Lace, an effect re-created here.

THE FISHPOND

The lower 'moat' is fed by a spring which bubbles up in the south-west corner of the garden. The reflections of the manor and the summer-house in its surface add further interest. Two medieval stewponds (used to keep fish for the table) were filled in to enlarge the orchards about 1890.

Above The summer-house was built by Sir Harold Brakspear

THE OWNERS OF GREAT CHALFIELD

THOMAS TROPNELL (*c.*1405–88): SELF-MADE SQUIRE

The Tropnells had long been minor gentry in north-west Wiltshire. As a young man, Thomas did legal work for the powerful Hungerford family, and through their influence was elected MP for Great Bedwin (1429–30) and Bath (1449). In the 1450s he prospered as a merchant trading through the thriving port of Bristol. During the upheavals of the Wars of the Roses, he was careful to stay friendly with both sides, surviving the execution of his patron, Robert, Lord Hungerford, in 1464. Tropnell gradually built up a large Wiltshire estate by purchase and by judicious marriages to Agnes Bourton and his kinswoman Margaret Ludlow. But in those uncertain times, establishing his right to his property involved long legal wrangles, at which he excelled. He was a persistent pragmatist, described in 1453 by one opponent as 'a perilous covetouse man'. In the Tropnell cartulary (to be displayed in the Great Hall) he set out at exhaustive length his legal claim to

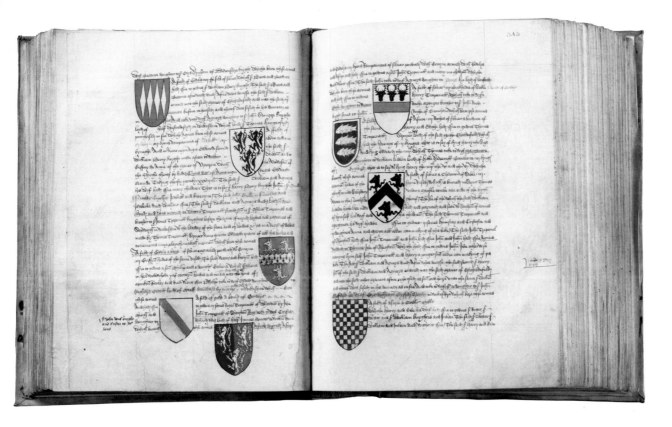

Great Chalfield, in part through his descent from Sir Harry de Percy, whose family had owned the estate since at least the 12th century. Tropnell had first bought an interest in Great Chalfield in 1437, but such was the legal confusion that he only felt confident enough to start building the new house 30 years later, when he was already an old man.

Tropnell chose the finest local craftsmen and materials, carting stone from a quarry at Hazelbury three miles to the north, which he had bought in 1465. Completed around 1480, Great Chalfield Manor was intended to cement Tropnell's hard-won status as a gentleman and an important figure in the county. His coat of arms and motto are prominently displayed on both the house and the church. He spent his final years here, but even in death he could not relax. He chose to be buried at Corsham, where he had lived previously, in a tomb he had designed for himself and his second wife.

Above The Tropnell cartulary, in which Tropnell meticulously documented his claim to Great Chalfield

OPPOSITE

Above The Dining Room mural is thought to depict Thomas Tropnell

Left The Tropnell coat of arms appears on the vaulting of the Great Hall bays and throughout the house

Right Tropnell employed the finest craftsmen to carve this head below the Solar oriel window and other decorative details

THE LATER TROPNELLS AND THE EYRES

Tropnell was succeeded by his son Christopher (d.1503), who probably built the Tudor service wing to the west of the main house. His last direct male heir was Giles Tropnell, who died young in 1553 in a freak hunting accident:

… as hunting, putting one end of a pair of dog couples [leads] over his head, running after his sport, and leaping over a hedge, the end of the dog couple which hung at his back took hold of a bough [and] kept him from touching the ground until he was strangled.

The estate was divided between Giles's sisters, Great Chalfield passing to the eldest, Ann, who in 1550 married John Eyre (d.1581), MP for Wiltshire and Salisbury. The Eyres were one of the oldest families in the county, but till then had been only minor gentry. In 1631 Ann's grandson, Sir John Eyre, sold Great Chalfield to Sir Richard Gurney, but Sir John retained a life interest in the property for his stepmother, Dame Ann, who was still living here when the Civil War broke out in 1642.

Below John and Anne Eyre's initials appear on the plasterwork they added to the dining room

THE CIVIL WAR

Between August 1644 and September 1646 Great Chalfield was occupied by a Parliamentary garrison of around 200 men and 100 horses, and in April 1645 it endured a brief siege by Royalist troops. The garrison strengthened the building's defences and fortified themselves by stocking up with 3½ hundredweight of cheese. They seem to have lived mainly on bread, cheese, bacon and beer, with the occasional fresh fish. (The garrison accounts record payments to mend a boat used for fishing in the moat.) Windows were smashed during the siege, but it is unclear how much other damage was done. In 1652 Gurney's executors tried to claim £2,000 in compensation, but this seems to have been an exaggeration.

STUART AND GEORGIAN GREAT CHALFIELD

In 1649 Gurney's widow sold Great Chalfield for £3,900 to Thomas Hanham the younger of Wimborne in Dorset. In 1673 it was sold again, to John Hall, who was a remote descendant of Tropnell and a wealthy clothier from Bradford-on-Avon, which he had endowed with almshouses. On his death in 1711, Hall left Great Chalfield to his granddaughter Rachael Baynton (1695–1722) of Little Chalfield. In a steep step up the social ladder, she married William Pierrepont, Earl of Kingston, but he died shortly afterwards, in 1713. The Earl was succeeded by his son, Evelyn, later 2nd Duke of Kingston. For the first time in its history, Great Chalfield was owned by a national figure – if only in the realm of Georgian scandal.

A scandalous marriage

The Duke of Kingston was a wealthy aristocrat, whose main estates were in Nottinghamshire, at Thoresby and Holme Pierrepont, but Great Chalfield was not forgotten: in 1752 he built a new barn in the farmyard, which is inscribed with a ducal 'K'.

About 1750 Kingston fell in love with Elizabeth Chudleigh, who became his mistress. She was already a notorious figure in high society: when George II had asked permission to place his hand on her breast, she had guided it to a softer place – the King's forehead! What the Duke did not know was that Elizabeth had clandestinely married Lord Hervey in 1744. When the marriage was revealed in court, she denied it. Kingston was so besotted that he believed her, and the couple were married in 1769. Both regretted it. According to the Duke's valet, he never enjoyed a week's happiness thereafter. When he died in 1773, the truth came out, and Elizabeth was convicted of bigamy in a sensational trial before the House of Lords.

19

Top *The married Maid of Honor*, or, *The Widow'd Wife and her two Husbands*. An engraving of 1775 inspired by Elizabeth Chudleigh's sensational trial for bigamy
Above Christopher Tropnell probably built the Tudor kitchen range, which connects the house with the 14th-century gatehouse

THE NEALES

Great Chalfield was bought in 1769 for £15,000 by Robert Neale of Shaw House, Melksham. Neale was a wealthy clothier and MP for Wootton Bassett. In 1775 he added the vestry to the church over a new burial vault for his family. On his death in 1776 he gave a life interest in the property to his granddaughter, Grace Elizabeth Neale.

In 1795 Grace married Harry Burrard (1765–1840), who took her surname. Burrard had entered the navy in 1778 at the age of thirteen and in a career spanning three wars and five decades he rose to be Admiral Sir Harry Burrard Neale, Baronet and MP for Lymington, where he is commemorated by a granite obelisk. Perhaps his finest hour came in 1797, when 'the influence of his exalted character kind but undaunted, mild but determined' (according to his monument) dissuaded the crew of his ship, HMS *San Fiorenzo*, from joining the mutiny at the Nore.

The Burrard Neales lived at his family home at Walhampton in Hampshire, and let out Great Chalfield to local farmers, but they maintained an interest in the place. With the house came the right to appoint the rector. In 1809 this was the Rev. Richard Warner, an industrious antiquarian and guidebook writer, whose sermons were said to have been 'models of pulpit eloquence'. In 1823 Burrard Neale commissioned John Buckler and his son to paint a series of six beautiful and informative watercolours of the house and church. Thirteen years later, he got the architect Thomas Larkins Walker, a pupil (and later friend and executor) of A.C. Pugin, to survey Great Chalfield. This seems to have been done with a view to restoration, but in the event the house was crudely altered by the tenant. (The south range had disappeared before 1794, and in 1838 much of the east wing was demolished.) However, Walker's drawings (published as the third series of Pugin's *Examples of Gothic Architecture* in 1837) were to prove an immensely valuable record of Thomas Tropnell's house.

Below Admiral Sir Harry Burrard Neale

Right T.L Walker's meticulous drawing of the gable-end figures

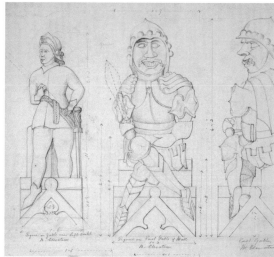

THE FULLERS

In 1878 Great Chalfield was sold once again, to G.P. Fuller of Neston Park, which had belonged to Thomas Tropnell four centuries before. Fuller was MP for Westbury, in 1894 leading the rescue of the Avon Rubber Company, which was one of the largest employers in Melksham. He became chairman of the company, a post he held until his death in 1927.

Like the Burrard Neales, Fuller let out the house: in 1901 the tenants were a farmer, James Bailey, his wife Anna Maria, son James, and two servants, Frances Dash and Maud Church.

The house was by now in a fairly dilapidated state, and Fuller seems to have contemplated further demolition, but fortunately the Baileys managed to dissuade him, because the tide was about to turn dramatically.

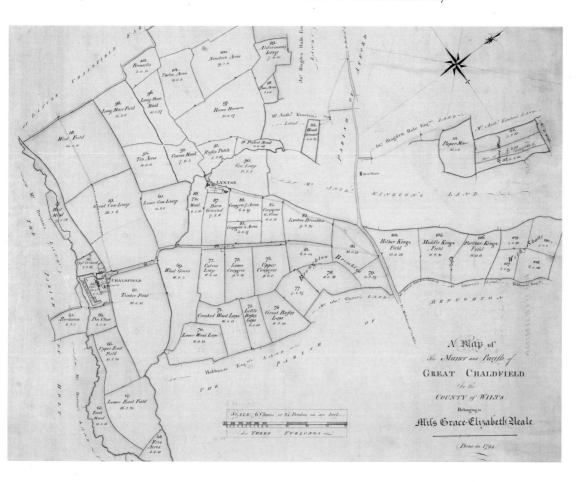

Above A watercolour of the manor house and church in 1886

Left The manor and parish of Great Chalfield in 1794

Right The Solar wing had to be largely rebuilt by Brakspear following T.L. Walker's drawings

EDWARDIAN REVIVAL

ROBERT FULLER

Robert was G.P. Fuller's fourth son. He trained as an electrical engineer, winning a gold medal at Faraday House in 1896. He also served in the Royal Wiltshire Yeomanry and became an alderman of Wiltshire County Council at an early age. In 1897 he joined Avon Rubber as works manager, becoming managing director and ultimately chairman in succession to his father. The company expanded rapidly in the late 1890s with the boom in demand for rubber tyres for bicycles and motor cars. By 1906 annual sales had topped £100,000.

Fuller had taken the fishing at Great Chalfield from his father for a shilling a year in 1903 and became very fond of the place. His success at Avon Rubber gave him the resources to contemplate a complete restoration of the house. Work started in 1905 under the guidance of the architect Sir Harold Brakspear. Brakspear proved an ideal choice. He lived locally and had a deep knowledge of Wiltshire's medieval buildings, having restored the ancient cloisters at Lacock Abbey. Working with Walker's measured drawings and fragments of the original stonework that still lay around the site, he was able to piece the house back together with admirable sensitivity. A century on, it is becoming increasingly difficult to distinguish old work from new. Brakspear also designed a series of new outbuildings to the west, including an engine-house for the waterworks, motor-houses, forge, stables, woodshed and potting shed.

In 1911 Major Fuller married Mabel Chappell, and although their new home was not yet quite finished, they moved in. The following year, he bought the house from his father, and together the Fullers set about refurnishing it with old oak pieces that would not only sit happily in such ancient interiors, but also create a comfortable family home. The result now has an Edwardian period charm of its own. Although Major Fuller gave the house, garden and immediate surroundings to the National Trust in 1943, Great Chalfield remains a family home, cherished by the Fullers' grandson, Robert Floyd, and his family.

Left Robert and Mabel Fuller at Great Chalfield in 1938

Below Great Chalfield has been welcoming visitors for over 60 years

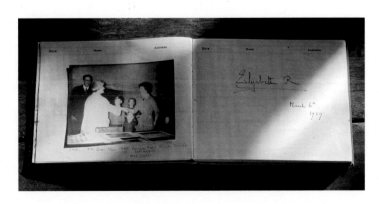